jargon watch

jargon watch

A pocket dictionary for the jitterati *

as Overheard by Gareth Branwyn

*1. What the digital generation becomes after tanking up on too much coffee
2. Fear and anxiety associated with not knowing the latest jargon, acronyms, and buzzwords of the Digital Revolution.

HARDWIRED
San Francisco

HardWired
520 Third Street, Fourth Floor
San Francisco, CA 94107

HardWired books are distributed to
the trade by Publishers Group West.

First Edition 1997
Printed in Singapore
10 9 8 7 6 5 4 3 2 1
ISBN 1-888869-06-2

Cover and Book Design
Susanna Dulkinys

Typography
A day (1996)
Designed by Susanna Dulkinys

FFLetter Gothic Text (1996)
Designed by Albert Pinggera based
on Monospaced Letter Gothic (1957)
designed by Roger Robertson

Introduction

It's untamed and anarchistic, with no central authority and no stuffy committees to answer to. Noses are frequently turned up whenever it's mentioned in high-brow circles. Much of its lexicon is off-putting to outsiders and newcomers. It has a funky mix of global and local voices, covering a staggering breadth of interests and trends. It can be poignant and inspirational or ridiculous and impenetrable. It's often riddled with hype and corporatespeak. A lot of it is infused with cleverness and great humor.

So, what is it? We could easily be describing the Internet, but we're talking about slang. It is perhaps no accident, though, that the two have so much in common. Even though lexicographers argue over what it is, slang has found an exploitable host within the world's high-speed communications networks, allowing it to overcome the traditional borders of close-knit interest groups and entrenched subcultures. Like a good joke, a newly expressed piece of viral slang can spread through interoffice email and over the Internet faster than a head cold through a kindergarten classroom. Good slang wants to be free.

Defining Our Terms

The word **slang** usually refers to informal, non-standard vocabulary coined by a social or special interest group (e.g., college students, skateboarders, drug dealers, NIN fans), whereas **jargon** is the special language of a technical profession (e.g., aviators, the military, computer geeks). Slang is often considered to be faddish, more short-lived than jargon.

The lexicon that is emerging from the digital cultures of the Internet has smudged the boundaries between jargon and slang. Some of the jargon of hackers and engineers (e.g., **FAQ, RAM, bandwidth, GUI**) has invaded popular language. Subcultural argot and techspeak once migrated slowly from one technical group to another because of the groups' relative insularity.

Now, with the interconnectivity of the wired world, slang and jargon quickly travel from one group or locale to another as they find useful niches elsewhere. Accelerated cross-pollination occurs through newsgroups, email, BBSes, Web pages, and trade shows. Jargon is also used as raw genetic material in Net slang, mutated in such terms as **ROM Brain**, **404**, and **CaptiveX**.

For the title of this book (and the **Wired** column that spawned it) we use the term **jargon**, although in truth, most of what it contains is technically slang. A precedent for this usage was set in hackerdom, where techie-infused slang has long been referred to as "the jargon." That term, and the well-known Jargon File that has circulated among geeks since the mid-'70s (later collected and expanded in Eric Raymond's **Hacker's Dictionary**), was one of the inspirations behind **Wired**'s Jargon Watch column. This book collects the terms published in that column from May 1993 to December 1996, as well as over 100 new entries. Jargon and slang speak volumes about the people who use them. Like a form of data compression, they can pack a tremendous amount of information — the values, ideas, anxieties, and humor of a subculture — into a single word or phrase. We can learn a lot about a subculture by decompressing its language. For instance, rummaging through the hacker lexicon reveals a cluster of related terms (called a **semantic field** in linguistics) describing computer sales and marketing people (**sales droids, sales critters, salesthings, market droids, marketeers, marketing slime**) and company management types in general (**suits, droids, stupids**). We find an equally large number of terms related to new and casual computer users (**lusers, lamers, wannabes, newbies, B1FFs, weenies, twinks, spods, tourists, read-only users**). College slang, not surprisingly, is rife with words relating to drinking and drugging (**blind, blitzed, trashed, toasted, greased, fried, blistered, ripped to the tits**). Rock climber slang has many words related to cuts (**flappers, gobbis**), falling (**to munge, to crater, peel**), and fear (**pucker factor, shaky legs**). Corporatespeak offers us such manglish as **calendaring** (scheduling), **audience development engines** (Web sites), **advertainment** (ads), and **new consumer paradigm** (market).

Where Do These Terms Come From?

One of the most common questions we get in the Jargon Watch email box is: "Do you all make this stuff up or what?" The answer is (mostly) no. We've collected these terms from online discussions and glossaries, Web pages, email submissions, trade shows and lectures, conversations with fellow geeks, magazines and newspapers, and TV news and computer programs. We also use a series of filters that scour newsgroups for keywords such as **jargon, slang, argot, lingo, colloquialism,** and **terminology**. In a few instances we've coined terms ourselves after having a "there's gotta be a word for that!" discussion (e.g., **egosurfing, idea hamster**).

So, how common are these words in actual usage? Some have become very popular since appearing in the magazine (**delurking, going postal, infobahn, Siliwood, Webmaster**). Many terms come from a certain subcultural orbit and stay there; others are not necessarily practical for everyday usage but were entertaining or illustrative enough to publish anyway. The Jargon Watch column has always been more about entertainment and humor than rigor and lexicographical correctness, more **Snigglets** than **Webster's**.

Whereas collections such as **The Hacker's Dictionary** take a more traditional linguistics approach, with etymologies, style notes, and historical anecdotes, Jargon Watch has mainly gone for entertainment and laughs. When someone submits a term, we're not overly concerned about its origins (although we prefer words that have established usage). If it strikes my fancy, I pass it down the editorial food chain. If after passing through all the editor's hands it hasn't been given the ax, I assume it's interesting and useful enough to get a shot in the magazine. I fancy myself a sort of slang impresario. If a term passes the editorial audition, I push it out onto the stage provided by the magazine. If it bombs, it gets the hook and its career is finished (or perhaps it ends up opening for a ventriloquist act in the Catskills). If it's a big success, it ends up making the rounds of email boxes, water coolers, and office cubicles, from Silicon Valley to **Silicon Alley** and beyond.

The words that made it into the column and this book are just a fraction of the terms submitted. Every week, dozens of terms pop into the Jargon Watch mailbox and get shuffled into three folders (A-list, B-list, and Jargon from Hell). Most of them end up in the latter two and never see ink. Over the years, I've acquired a perverse fascination with the hellish terms that have that so-bad-they're-good quality. Here are a few of the scarier ones:

anticipointment
chronolibrium
e-gasm
gratuitml
infojaculation   •
inventrepreneur
javangelist
medtigious
nintendomaniaddictionitis
pageversationalist
pornetgraphy
Webference

Can't you just picture the hapless **jargonauts** sitting in their Dilbertesque cubicles cutting and pasting the English language in a vain attempt to see their names in print? I weed these out of my mailbox each week, trying to keep my sanity intact while looking for those illusive gems that make it all worthwhile. The week in which I write this has just offered up **blamestorming, prairie dogging,** and **tract mansions.**

More Jargon Watching

Most of us know more jargon and slang than we can recall when asked about it. As I circulate through parties, trade shows, and cyberspace, I always ask people about the jargon and slang they use. Usually, they can't think of much off the top of their heads, but they'll often email me afterward. Frequently used cant disappears into the fabric of our lives, and only professional and armchair linguists (and editors of jargon columns) are obsessed with teasing those threads back out. I hope this dictionary will inspire you to examine the in-group language you use and to type some into an email message and send it to us at **jargon@wired.com** (with "jargon" in the subject). We're especially looking for words related to all the diverse niches of media, digital culture, business, and emerging sciences and technology. We'll also take a look at any neologisms related to life in the post-Gutenberg era. Please don't just sit around trying to invent terms to submit. If you think up a word you like, try it out on your friends and cubicle mates and see if it catches on. The good stuff will quickly take on a life of its own.

To participate in the evolving lexicon of this book and the Jargon Watch column, check out our Web page at **www.jargonwatch.com/**.

Gareth Branwyn
February 1997

Acknowledgments

So many people have contributed to **Wired**'s Jargon Watch column and this book that it is probably impossible to thank them all (but I'll try).

First off, I should thank Kevin Kelly for giving me the gig. He recognized my interest in the lexicon of cyberculture and dreamed up the idea for the Jargon Watch column. I'd also like to acknowledge those who piqued my interest in jargon and slang in the first place: William Gibson (via his slang-ridden cyberpunk novels), the early hacker's **Jargon File** and Eric S. Raymond's subsequent **Hacker's Dictionary**, Doug Coupland (**Generation X**), Connie Eble (**College Slang 101**), and Rich Hall (**Snigglets**).

Everyone at **Wired** (especially Scan editors Mark Frauenfelder and Todd Lappin) and **Wired UK** gets a tip o' the propeller beanie, along with Connie Hale and the editors of **Wired Style**, the folks at HardWired, especially Hollis Heimbouch,

Donna Linden, copy editor Alan Titche, **Jargon Watch** designer Susanna Dulkinys, and typesetter Darren R. David. High fives also go to the friends and family members that fax, email, or call me with new terms they uncover. Finally, I'd like to thank the hundreds of jargonauts who weekly toss stuff into the jargon mailbox. Those whose submissions proved viral (i.e., were published in the column and/or this book) are listed in the Credits.

®☼ℒℒ the ©redits

Rami Ahonen, Dan Amrich, Orrin Anderson,
Andrew Anker, Reva Basch, John Battelle, John
Bergin, RuthAnne Bevier, Ralph Bishop, Pierre
Bourque, Hugh Brackett, Stewart Brand, Liz
Brown, Mark C, Arnie Cachelin, Fraser Cain, Sean
Carton, Steven Cherry, Clark4416, Simon Clark,
codeHound, Gary Coffman, Anne-Marie
Conception, Stuart Constanine, Doug Coupland,
Jim Crawley, Jack Croyd, Jennifer Dalton,
Philippe Dambournet, Charles Daniels, Rick
Deluxe, Patrick Dirks, Steve Doberstein, Jim
Drewry, Jerry Dunn, Matisse Enzer, FionaM945,
Mike Fisher, Sharon Fisher, Jim Flanagan, Joe
Flower, Jesse Freund, Adam Ford, Bruce Francis,
Mark Frauenfelder, Alberto Gaitan, GardnerIV,
Jill Gillham, Peter Goggin, Michael Gold, David
Goldberg, Adrienne Greenheart, D. Scott
Gregory, Justin Hall, Mikki Halpin, Patrick
Harrington, Martin Hardee, Arno Harris, J. C.
Herz, James Higa, John Holland, Mike Hrusecky,
Tom Igoe, Marjorie Ingall, Ian Iver, Gavin Ivester,

Jamie and Jeanne, Mike Jennings, Tom Jennings, Chicago Joe, JohnR470, Carl Kadie, Dan Kalowsky, Alan Kay, Tom Kelleher, Kevin Kelly, Molly E. Ker, Garth Kidd, James Kim, Leif Knutsen, Will Kreth, Bob Lai, Steve Lamsens, Todd Lappin, Rebecca Lartigue, Alan Lasoff, Robert Lauriston, David Lawrence, Scott Lawrence, Jon Lebkowsky, Darryl Lee, Jim Leftwich, Laura Lemay, Andrew Leonard, Linda Lewett, Ernest Limperis, Keith Loh, Brian Maggi, Karl Mamer, Doug Manchester, John Manning, Kevin Marks, Jules Marshall, Stanton McCandlish, Joel McLemore, Jeffrey P. McManus, Brock Meeks, Melchionda, Jane Metcalfe, Mike Mikula, Destry Miller, Drue Miller, misterskin, Laura Mitchell, Daniel Modell, Tony Mosa, Eugene Mosier, Daniel A. Murphey, Peter A. Ndenga, Michael Newman, Nicol, Monty Nicol, Bruce Oberg, Patrick O'Connell, Ann Okerson, Sheila O'Shea, Jonelle Patrick, Davo Perry, Ted Peters, John Pettitt, Dan Pink, Jef Poskanzer, Brian Quennell, Joshua Quittner, Kit Ranshoff, Mitchell Rasor, Steve Read, Steve Rhodes, Steve Roby,

Corey Rosen, Gary Rosenzweig, Louis Rossetto, Robert Rossney, Peter Rothman, Thomas D. Russell, Eric Schlachter, Karl Schmidtmann, Erich Schrempp, Philippe Scoffie, Dan "Sleepy" Sears, Jef Sewell, John Shirley, Ward Shrake, Steve Silberman, Aaron Simpson, Carla Sinclair, Jeet Singh, David Smith, Mark Smith, Ray Smith, Andy Snevets, Elliot Sobel, Kristin Spence, Ross Alan Stapleton, Brett Stephens, Bruce Sterling, Peter Sugarman, John Raymond Sumser, Etienne Tasse, Tarik Thami, Eric S. Theise, Mandy Thomas, Nick Topolos, Jean F. Trudel, Claudia Tucker, Bruce Turkel, Alan Turner, Tyson Vaughan, Howard Wen, Jessica Wing, Shawn Wolfe.

ABCD
Acronym coined immediately after the ABC/Disney deal.

Adminisphere
The rarefied organizational layers beginning just above the rank and file. Decisions that fall from the adminisphere are often profoundly inappropriate or irrelevant to the problems they were designed to solve.

Advocacy Stats
Statistics assembled or championed by advocates of a cause with little regard for their accuracy.

Allianceware
See **Coopetition**.

Alpha Geek

The most knowledgeable, technically proficient person in an office or work group. "Ask Larry, he's the alpha geek around here."

America Off-Line

The new nickname for AOL as it struggles to keep up with constant growth spurts and as system slowdown reaches an all-time high.

Ant Farm

One of those huge multiscreen theater complexes with a glass facade found throughout America's mall belts. Also called a "gigaplex." See also **Generica**.

Anus Envy

The condition common among fans of The Jerky Boys, Howard Stern, Rush Limbaugh, and others trying to emulate (or outdo) their idols.

Appeasement Engineer

The field service engineer whose job is to arrive at your site within the guaranteed response time, make sure the machine is plugged in, and then call the home office for further instructions.

Architecture Police

An individual or group within a company that makes sure software-hardware development follows established corporate guidelines. The architecture police are also used to rein in excessively creative development efforts in conservative organizations.

Arrow Shooters
The visionaries in an organization who come up with ideas and trace their far-reaching trajectories. See also **Road Builders**.

Articulizer
The device through which certain radio news organizations (such as NPR) must feed interviews to make everyone come out sounding thoughtful and articulate. Also called the "de-UMMer."

AssGrabber
A more honest name for FileGrabber, AOL's binary file decoder most widely used for viewing newsgroup porno.

Assmosis

The process by which some people seem to absorb success and advancement by kissing up to the boss rather than working hard.

Astroturf Campaign

A fake grassroots political campaign. Not to be confused with **glassroots campaign.**

Balloon Help

What you get when someone insists on explaining every obvious detail and function of an electronic device. Refers to the rarely used Balloon Help feature on Macs. "Um...I don't really need balloon help, just give me the domain address."

Bambi

What game and talk show staffers call someone who freezes in front of the camera (like a deer caught in headlights).

Bandwidth Junkie

One who worships brute speed when it comes to Internet connections – the type of person who has a leased line in his/her bedroom.

Barfogenesis

That seasick feeling some people get when using virtual reality headsets. Caused by a conflict in the brain: the eyes register movement, but the inner ear doesn't feel it. More commonly called "VR sickness."

Barker Channel

An all-previews video channel.

Barney Page

Web page designed to capitalize on a trend (such as Barney bashing). "Have you seen all the macarena Barney pages?"

Batmobiling

Putting up protective emotional shields just as a relationship enters an intimate, vulnerable stage. Refers to the retracting armor covering the Batmobile.

Battle Faxes
Rounds of vitriolic faxes between clients and their lawyers, fighting lovers, or the like. "Here are the latest battle faxes with the lawyers at my record company."

Beeper Sitting
To assume responsibility for recording all incoming pages and encoded messages for a vacationing or otherwise out-of-range friend who owns a beeper. "Rebecca is beeper sitting for Jennifer while she's in Florida."

Beepilepsy
The brief seizure people sometimes have when their beeper goes off (especially in vibrator mode). Characterized by physical spasms, goofy facial expressions, and interruption of speech in midsentence.

Begathon

A TV or radio fund-raiser for a charity, religious organization, or PBS station in which every form of guilt, sweet-talking, and outright begging is used to get people to fork over dough.

Betamaxed

When a technology is overtaken by an inferior, but better marketed, technology. "Apple was betamaxed out of the market by Microsoft."

Bicycle Networking

The practice among cable access TV shows of distributing programming from one local cable access station to another.

Bio-break

Techie euphemism for having to use the toilet. See also **BRB**.

Biots

Mobile artificial agents that can sense a simulated environment, interact (signaling, mating, food finding) with other biots, and learn and evolve over time. From BioLand, a UCLA experiment in developing distributed forms of intelligence using massively parallel computing.

Bi Star
[from "Binary Star Configuration"]

Any grouping of two things that are seemingly inseparable, for whatever reason. "Tattoos and piercings: totally bi star!"

Bit Diddling

The act of manipulating bits with little to show for it. "The artist bit diddled the image for hours, but I can't see much of an improvement." See also **Rasterbator.**

Bit Flip
A 180° personality change. "Jim did a major bit flip and became a born-again Christian."

Bitloss
The loss of databits during a transmission. Also used colloquially to mean loss of memory or information. See also **Blowing Your Buffer.**

Bitnik
Someone who uses a public, coin-operated computer terminal to log onto the Internet.

Bitraking [from "muckraking"]
Net-based investigative journalism.

Bitslag
All the useless rubble one must plow through on the Net to get to the rich information ore. See also **Slag.**

Bit-spit
Any form of digital correspondence (text, bit-mapped images, fax transmissions) or the act of sending same. "Did you bit-spit that file to Jane yet?"

Black Widow
A Java applet that, when executed, does destructive things to one's computer. Also called a "malicious applet." See also **Crapplet**.

Blamestorming
Sitting around in a group discussing why a deadline was missed or a project failed and who is responsible. Like brainstorming, from which it is derived, blamestorming is done with little regard for the quality of the contribution to the discussion.

Blendo

The combination of lots of different media from a variety of sources (type, computer graphics, scanned imagery, animation, video). Similar to multimedia, but more often used to describe a collage/kitchen-sink approach. Can also refer to static images that have these combined elements. Also called "meltomedia."

BLOB [Binary Large Object]

Used to describe very large binary files. "The speed of your server is a function of the size and number of BLOBs you'll be moving through the network." According to **The Hacker's Dictionary**, this term is also used to mean **mail bombing** someone with a very large file.

Blowing Your Buffer

Losing one's train of thought. Occurs when the person you're speaking with won't let you get a word in edgewise, and/or has just said something so astonishing that your train gets derailed. "Damn, I just blew my buffer!" See also **Bitloss**.

Body Nazis

Hardcore exercise and weight-lifting fanatics who look down on anyone who doesn't obsessively work out. See also **Exercise Bulimics**.

Bookmark

To take note of a person for future reference (borrowing from the Web browser metaphor). "I bookmarked him after I saw his cool demo at Siggraph."

Botrunner

A person who operates software robots on the Net.

Bots [short for "robots"]

Little programs designed to perform automated tasks on the Internet (such as indexing) and to act as human surrogates. On IRC (Internet Relay Chat), bots can be malicious, cloning themselves (clonebots) or flooding the IRC channel with garbage (floodbots). There are hundreds of different types of bots: cancelbots, chatterbots, softbots, userbots, taskbots, sloth bots, and Xbots.

One of the earliest, most notorious bots of Usenet legend is the ZumaBot (or ArgicBot). From 1993 to 1994, an "entity" named Serdar Argic began posting long messages containing pro-Turkish, anti-Armenian propaganda to certain newsgroups. No one knows whether Argic was in fact a robot or a human with too much time on his hands (or a combination of both), but the legend of the ZumaBot was assured when a posting about turkey casserole was answered by an Argic screed.

Bottom-lining

What phone and cable companies consider when picking areas for trials and early deployment of interactive services. They look for areas full of upper- and upper middle-class households with enough money to pay for these services and generally ignore areas with lower incomes.

Bozon

A unit of stupidity. "Is it just me, or is there always a high bozon count in Rupert's posts?"

Brain Fart

1. The result of mental indigestion (called a "braino" in hacker slang) that causes one to make an embarrassing mistake. For example, trying to fast-forward a real-time TV program after watching videotaped programming.
2. A by-product of a bloated mind, producing information effortlessly. A burst of useful information. "I know you're busy on the Microsoft story, but could you give us a brain fart on the Mitnik bust?"

When we published **brain fart** in **Wired 3.06,** we used the second definition and made reference to the first. I was flamed in email by several hackers who took offense at the changed usage. I'd gotten the new usage from someone in the CNBC newsroom. Its **bit flip** was probably due to someone hearing the term but not the meaning…so one was made up to preserve the term. Jargon/slang is very viral this way. **Brain fart** even found its way onto Bill Maher's **Politically Incorrect.**

Brandwidth

The theoretical limit of a product's expandability into different media, market segments, and so on. "Hello Kitty has a shockingly large brandwidth."

BRB [Be Right Back]

Used in chat rooms when users' avatars (online graphic personae) remain on-screen while users do something else. See also **Bio-break.**

Break a Meg

Hollywired mutation of the ol' show biz "Break a leg!"

Brilliant Weapons

Military term for the next generation of weapons systems beyond "smart," such as those based on nanotechnology. See also **Fire Ant Warfare.**

Byte-bonding

Occurs when computer users get together and discuss things that noncomputer users don't understand. When byte-bonded people start playing on a computer during a noncomputer-related social situation, they are "geeking out."

CaptiveX

Pejorative term for Microsoft's ActiveX language (because it holds software developers and corporate information system managers captive to a proprietary system).

Carbon Community [CC]

The "real" community a person lives in. His/her geographical, as opposed to virtual, neighbors. See also **Meatspace**.

Career-limiting Maneuver [CLM]

Used to describe an ill-advised activity. Sending one's boss a memo on recycled paper, the reverse of which contains a rant against him/her, is a serious CLM (a real-life example, btw).

CEOP-phobia
The male fear of peeing while standing next to one's CEO at a urinal.

CGI Joe
A hardcore CGI programmer who has all the social skills and charisma of a plastic action figure.

Chain Saw Consultants
Outside experts brought in to reduce the employee headcount (leaving the top brass with clean hands).

Chamber Art
Term coined by electronic music composer Morton Subotnick (creator of the CD-ROM art piece **All My Hummingbirds Have Alibis**) to refer to the intimate one-on-one relationship that an artist can have with an audience through computer-based art.

Chaord

A self-organizing, adaptive, nonlinear complex system (whether physical, biological, or social) that simultaneously exhibits characteristics of order and chaos. A system that exists between regulatory rigidity and flexibility.

Cheetos Syndrome

That strange empty feeling one gets after pigging out on too many nutritionless (but brightly colored!) Web pages.

Chip Jewelry

A euphemism for old computers destined to be scrapped or turned into chip and circuit board jewelry. "I paid three grand for that Mac SE and now it's nothing but chip jewelry."

Chips and Salsa
Chips = hardware, salsa = software.
"Well, first we gotta figure out if the problem's in your chips or your salsa."

Churn
A section of computer code that is forever being rewritten or changed. Text documents can also have churn. Anything written by a committee is rife with churn.

Circling the Drain
Medical slang for a patient near death who refuses to give up the ghost. Used generally to describe projects that have no more life in them but refuse to die. "That disk conversion project has been circling the drain for years."

Clickstreams

The paths a user takes when navigating cyberspace. Advertisers and online media learn valuable consumer surfing habits by tracking users' clickstreams.

Client/Server Action

Geek euphemism for getting laid. "I went to the Oracle party the other night hoping for a little client/server action."

Coasters

1. Unsolicited floppy disks, such as the ubiquitous AOL software, that arrive in one's mailbox on a regular basis.
2. One-off CDs that get lost to a burn error, rendering them totally useless for everything except putting your coffee on (or reshingling your roof).
See also **Disk Dancers.**

Coþшεb

A World Wide Web site that hasn't been updated for a long time. A dead Web page.

CodεPiε

1. A pizza that one orders while writing code. 2. The pizza one orders to celebrate the compiling of said code. 3. The code itself, tastefully and elegantly organized.

Cof$

Abbreviation for the Church of Scientology, used by its detractors on the alt.religion.scientology newsgroup. In hackerdom, CI$ refers to CompuServe Information Service.

Cold Transfer

An incoming phone call transferred without notice or explanation from the transferring party. "Someone in customer service cold transferred the call to me — by that point the guy was ready to crawl through the wires and kill somebody."

Coopetition

The phenomenon of computer companies joining their competitors on a project-by-project basis. The products, when there are actual products, are called "allianceware."

Cornea Gumbo

A visually noisy, overdesigned Photoshopped mess. "Gawd, we've got to redesign that page, it's become total cornea gumbo." See also **Rasterbator**.

Crapplet

A badly written or profoundly useless Java applet. "I just wasted 30 minutes downloading this stinkin' crapplet!" See also **Black Widow**.

Crash Edit

Low-budget video editing done using only a camcorder and a consumer video deck (as opposed to professional editing equipment).

Crash Test Dummies

Those of us who pay for unstable, not-ready-for-prime-time software foisted on us by greedy computer companies.

Critical Mess
An unstable stage in a software project's life in which any single change or bug fix can result in the creation of two or more new bugs. Continued development at this stage leads to an exponential increase in the number of bugs.

Cross-roasting
Following up a message posted to a Usenet newsgroup by adding one or more additional groups to the response in an effort to bring the original post to the attention of those likely to flame it. For example, in a follow-up to a particularly over-the-top feminist rant, a cross-roaster might add alt.mens-rights and soc.men.

Cube Farm
An office filled with cubicles. See also **Prairie Dogging.**

Culture Jamming
Term coined by the audio collage band Negativland to refer to billboard altering and other forms of media sabotage (postering, media hoaxing, guerilla art actions, etc.).

Cumdex
Nickname for the "adult technology" sideshow that spun off from Comdex after trade show officials were pressured to exclude porno exhibitors.

Cusskiddie
AOL cybercop-speak for an immature user who posts vulgarity in a public forum. "You've got a cusskiddie in the SNES vs. Genesis forum."

Cyberluddites

Net users who are against the World Wide Web and Net commercialism and who want to return to all text-based communications. An organization called Reclaim the Networks! is leading the cyberluddite charge.

Cyber Noir

Used to describe dark, trippy, weird "cyber" films and TV shows like **Wild Palms, Tank Girl,** and **VR.5.**

Cyberpork

Government money flowing to well-connected information superhighway contractors.

Cybersitters

Young, underemployed, computer literates who "sit" with rich kids, teaching them how to surf the Internet and create multimedia graphics.

This term was sent to Jargon Watch by the cybersitter of William Gibson's son Graeme.

Cyberwar

See **Infowar.**

Cybrarian

A digital librarian. One who makes his/her living doing online research and information retrieval.

ÐAGs [Ðata Acquisition Geeks]

Name for the pit crew members who monitor a race car's computer systems.

Ðancing Baloney

Little animated GIFs and other Web F/X that are useless and serve simply to impress clients. "This page is kinda dull. Maybe a little dancing baloney will help." See also **Cornea Gumbo**, **Paintmonkey**, and **Rasterbator**.

Ðark Fiber

When a company lays high-bandwidth fiber-optic cable containing much more potential that can be currently used, the wire is said to be "dark." Not only are the telcos laying dark fiber, but so are oil and gas utilities companies, since they own long stretches of hollow pipe. See also **Pulling Glass**.

Datafreight

The long-haul transportation of bits in bulk. Any corporation with cross-country rights-of-way can get into the datafreight biz by laying fat fiber. See also **Pulling Glass.**

Data Mining

What companies with huge computers do with their databases. Extracting value (money) from the seemingly useless bedrock of numbers, statistics, and information.

Dawn Patrol

Programmers who are still at their terminals when the day shift returns to work the next morning.

Ðead End Users [ÐEUs]
A derogatory play on "end users." Used by some technical support people to refer to the clueless masses who call with painfully obvious tech questions.

Ðead Tree Edition
The paper version of a publication available in both paper and electronic forms, as in "the dead tree edition of the **San Francisco Chronicle**..." See also **Treeware.**

Ðeath Star Villages
Suburbs around New Jersey where many AT&T employees live. Makes reference to the AT&T logo, which employees have dubbed "The Death Star" (from the **Star Wars** films).

Deboning
The act of removing stitched-in
subscription cards, cardstock ad pages,
and "blow-in" cards from a magazine
to make it easier to read.

Decruitment
A corporate euphemism for laying off
workers. See also **Uninstalled.**

Delurking
Coming out of online "lurking mode,"
usually motivated by an irresistible
need to flame about something. "I just
had to delurk and add my two cents
to that conversation about the
Singapore caning."

Demo Dollies
The spokesmodels, usually women but sometimes men, who staff technology trade show booths and are obviously not chosen for their vast knowledge of the projects they are presenting.

Demunchkinization
Restoring vocal timbral characteristics after pitch-shifting audio recordings. Spotted in an Opcode press release.

Depotphobia
Fear associated with entering a Home Depot (or similar building supply store) because of how much money one might spend. Electronics geeks experience Shackophobia.

Ðesignosaurs
A species, nearing extinction, of designers who refuse to use computers.

Ðe-UMMer
See **Articulizer**.

Ðial Group
People who are gathered into a focus group and are given an electronic dial. As the group watches a speech or commercial, each person adjusts the device in a "feel negative about" or "feel positive about" direction. The group average is plotted on a fever chart that records a collective second-by-second judgment on the presentation. Dial groups are now commonly used for engineering political speeches.

Digital Watermark

A unique identifier that becomes part of a digital document and cannot be removed. The data is invisible, but a computer can analyze the document (such as an image) and pull out the hidden data.

Dilberted

To be exploited, oppressed, and screwed over by one's boss. Derived from the experiences of Dilbert, the geek-in-hell comic strip character. "I've been Dilberted again. The ol' man revised the software specs for the fourth time this week." The corresponding adjective is "Dilbertesque."

Disk Dancers

People, usually teenagers, who use the free AOL disks given away in magazines and via direct mail to hop from one free account to another, never having to pay to be online. See also **Coasters**.

Docubug

A mistake in computer documentation. The technical writing department at Sun Microsystems is called the "DocuZoo."

Dog Bones

The bone-shaped holographic stickers used to seal CD boxes. The term is also used in amateur radio to refer to a type of bone-shaped antenna insulator.

Domain Dipping

Typing in random words between **www.** and **.com** just to find out what's out there. See also **Serendipity Search**.

Domain Dropping

Giving someone you want to impress your hippest email address regardless of whether that's where you usually pick up your mail. "Kevin is such a domain dropper. He gives people his Well address, but he actually picks up his mail on AOL."

Domainism

Internet prejudice. Judging others on the basis of how cool/uncool their email address is. See also **Domain Dropping.**

Dot-Comify

The practice of "netifying" any word or phrase by adding **.com** to the end of it (e.g., **getalife.com**).

Drill Down

To navigate a series of hyperlinks through successive levels of data. "Go to the Olympics site and drill down to the Track and Field page." Also used generally to refer to tunneling into a large body of data.

Drop Paper

To make a firm purchasing agreement. "No one has dropped paper on it yet, but we have several likely prospects."

Dual-channelers

People who get all their information by channel-flipping between MTV and CNN.

Dustbuster

A phone call or email message sent to someone after a long silence just to "shake the dust off" and see if the connection still works.

Egosurfing

Scanning the Net, databases, print media, research papers, and so on, looking for references to one's own name.
See also **Masthead Envy.**

This is a term that is frequently submitted to Jargon Watch (along with variations such as "egofiltering"). The fascinating thing is that we know this term originated with **Wired.** It was coined by Sean Carton, an interactive media specialist from Baltimore. Sean and I were on the phone talking about things that need a word for them (such as using search engines to hunt down references to oneself). He called back several minutes later and blurted out "egosurfing!" So, it's particularly gratifying when this message in a bottle, tossed into the digital oceans of cyberspace, is repeatedly returned to us.

8th-Floor Decision

Refers to the 8th floor at the FCC, where the commissioner's offices and meeting rooms are located. Decisions made on the 8th floor have a profound effect on new communication services.

EJ [or E-jay]
An announcer for audio programming "netcast" through cyberspace.

Electronic Puppets
See **Synthespians**.

Eliza Effect
The tendency to believe that a computer has personality or intelligence when obviously it doesn't. Refers to an early computer program (called Eliza) that simulated a psychologist.

Elvis Year
The peak year of something's popularity. "Barney the dinosaur's Elvis year was 1993."

Email Tennis

When you email someone who responds while you're still answering mail. You respond again, and so forth, as if you are carrying on a chat via email messages. "OK, enough of this email tennis, why don't I call you?"

EMG

Acronym for "Empty Magnanimous Gesture," as in "We think your idea is great and would love to fund it, but [insert EMG here]."

Emotags

Mock HTML tags (<smile>, <smirk>, </smirk>) used in email and newsgroups in place of ASCII emoticons. "<flame> Someone tell that jerk to shut up, I'm getting sick of his vapid whining! </flame>."

Encrypted English

International correspondence from someone whose command of the English language is well intentioned, but tenuous. "We will most please thank you for investigating our problem in your computer."

Entertainmentization

Reduction in function, capabilities, and price of a sophisticated consumer product in an effort to expand its market (e.g., making a computer more like a television or gamebox).

Entrenched Transactors

Bank jargon for people who refuse to bank by ATM or computer, thus wasting the bank's money/time on tellers.

E-pursε [for "εlεctronic pursε"]
An electronic monetary transaction card or software. Also called "e-wallet."

E-tɑiling
Another one of those dubious "e-" abbreviations. This one is for "electronic retailing."

Eurominutεs
Scenes in a syndicated TV show that appear in the foreign version but are cut from U.S. episodes to increase the time available for commercials. "The scene where Rachel gets to Paris is only in the eurominutes."

E-wɑllεt
See E-purse.

Exercise Bulimics

People who compulsively work out after eating, and gauge each workout by how many calories they need to expend to burn off the food they just ate.
See also **Body Nazis.**

Extranet

A corporate intranet extended to bring in clients and suppliers.

Eyeballs

Media slang for a viewing audience. "There are plenty of new eyeballs available in this time slot."

Facetime

Spending time in person with someone mainly known online. "I'm going to New York City to have some facetime with the Echo folks." See also **F2F, Meatspace,** and **RL.**

Fast Tracking

In architecture, when design and construction documents for a building are just days ahead of the actual construction.

FAWOMFT [Frequently Argued Waste Of My F***ing Time]

A recurring argument that, like the Energizer Bunny, keeps going, and going, and going. "All the noise on alt.cyberpunk over whether William Gibson has an email address is a FAWOMFT."

Fine Business

Amateur radio slang used to fill dead air space or as an acknowledgment. Like "um" or "OK" in normal conversation.

Fire Ant Warfare

Theoretical weapons systems in which millions of small, smart weapons would swarm a target. See also **Brilliant Weapons.**

Firefighters

Net users who try to put out "flame wars" early in their gestation.

Fix It In Post

Used in video production to mean "we [or somebody else] will deal with this in postproduction." Sometimes used as an excuse to get out of a sticky situation, to postpone the agony of confronting any serious production problem.

Flash Crowds

Swarms of users on a computer network who appear, then disappear, in a flash. The term originates from a short story of the same name by Larry Niven. In the story, riots break out when thousands of people pour out of teleportation booths to see major social events.

Flight Risk

Used to describe employees who are suspected of planning to leave a company or department soon.

Floodgaters

Individuals who send you email inquiries and, after receiving only a slightly favorable response, begin flooding you with multiple messages of little or no interest.

Forelash [opposite of "backlash"]

Negative or indifferent reactions to nonexistent but already overhyped technologies, including video-on-demand, 500 channels, interactive TV, and anything promised in the AT&T "You Will" ads.

404

Someone who's clueless. From the World Wide Web error message "404 Not Found," meaning that the requested document could not be located. "Don't bother asking him...he's 404, man."

Franco-Bohemian

Business franchises presenting a commercial, sanitized slant on some corner of bohemian culture. Starbuck's, Kinko's, Ben & Jerry's, and Lollapalooza are franco-bohemian enterprises.

Frankenedit

A gruesome job of editing a writer's work by an editor in a hurry. The frankenedited piece is usually returned with a note asking the writer to suture it all back together and to breath life back in it (by the next morning).

Friday Night Pizza Maker [from Japan]

Someone who gets drunk after work and leaves a puddle of vomit on the subway platform.

F2F

Online shorthand for a "face-to-face" encounter instead of an online interaction. See also **Facetime**, **Meatspace**, and **RL**.

Fuel Fleas

Dust-sized pieces from the fuel rods in nuclear power plants. They float through the air, settling on clothing and, if you're unlucky, in your lungs.

Furverts

The denizens of FurryMUCK and alt.fan.furry or, in general, people who enjoy emulating anthropomorphs (humanoid animals). Not to be confused with the people who post on alt.sex.bestiality.

Future-proof

Term used to describe a phone system (or any technology) that supposedly won't become technologically outdated (at least anytime soon).

Gang FAQ

The act of group emailing an FAQ to others after they've asked a particularly stupid or old question on a newsgroup. Differs from a **mail bomb** in that each person sends only one copy, but numerous members of a newsgroup participate. See also **BLOB.**

Geekosphere

The area surrounding one's computer, where little trinkets, personal mementos, toys, and **monitor pets** are displayed. The place where computer geeks can show their "colors."

Geeksploitation

Taking advantage of twenty-something digital workers flushed with pioneer enthusiasm and willing to work long hours if bolstered by junk food, flexible schedules, and no dress code. A growing complaint in **Silicon Valley** and **Hollywired**.

Genεricα
Features of the American landscape (strip malls, motel chains, prefab housing) that are exactly the same no matter where one is. "We were so lost in generica, I actually forgot what city we were in." See also **Ant Farm**.

Gigαplεx
See **Ant Farm**.

Glαss
In aviation, a "glass" aircraft is one that has a digital cockpit, as opposed to a "steam gauge" or "rope start" cockpit with analog instruments. "Since moving up to glass, I never want to fly an ol' steam gauge machine again."

Glassroots Campaign

Grassroots campaigning conducted over the Internet. The EFF's and CPSR's online campaigns against the Clipper Chip and the CDA are prime examples. See also **Astroturf Campaign**.

Glazing

Corporatespeak for sleeping with one's eyes open. Popular pastime at many conferences and early morning meetings. "Didn't he notice that half the room was glazing by the second session?"

Glueware

The trend of tying software applications to physical networks through the AT&T system (e.g., the deal AT&T and Novell struck to adapt Novell local area networking software to communicate over AT&T's long-distance network).

Going Cyrillic

When a graphical display (LED panel, bit-mapped text and graphics) starts to display garbage. "The thing just went cyrillic on me."

Going Postal

Euphemism for being totally stressed out, for losing it. Makes reference to the unfortunate track record of postal employees who have snapped and gone on shooting rampages.

Going postal is the hands-down winner of the most submitted term to the Jargon Watch column. Strangely enough, after its initial appearance in the February 1994 issue of **Wired**, it took almost another year before we got further submissions of it. Now, we get one every couple of months. **Go postal** was used in the 1995 film **Clueless**.

Golden Rolodex

The small handful of experts who are always quoted in news stories and asked to be guests on discussion shows. "Henry Kissinger seems to be in the Golden Rolodex under foreign policy."

GOOD Job

A "Get-Out-Of-Debt" job. A well-paying job people take in order to pay off their debts, one that they will quit as soon as they are solvent again.

Goofcore

The constellation of rock subgenres that mix hardcore punk with things like polka, lounge music, and big doses of nerdy humor. New York's Black Velvet Flag, who did lounge versions of "classic" punk tunes, is one example of a goofcore group.

Graybar Land

The place one goes while staring at a computer that's slowly processing something (watching the gray progress bar crawl across the screen). "I was in graybar land for what seemed like hours thanks to that CAD rendering." Compare with **Render Wander**.

Gray Matter

Older, experienced businesspeople hired by young entrepreneurial firms so as to appear more reputable and established.

Guru Site

A superuseful, link-heavy Web site that's been put together by someone passionate about a particular subject. Net supersearcher Reva Basch writes: "Finding a guru site in the area you're researching is like stumbling across a consultant or research librarian and tapping into their expertise, for free. A tremendous shortcut, if you're lucky." See also **Cybrarian.**

Gutter Tribes

Nomadic bands of homeless people in their teens and early twenties who travel from city to city, making their living primarily by panhandling.

Hacker Tourism

Travel to exotic locations in search of sights and sensations that only a technogeek could love. The term was coined by Neal Stephenson in his colossal article for **Wired 4.12** on FLAG, a fiber-optic cable now being built from England to Japan.

Hand Salsa

The slimy substance invariably left over on a game controller or joystick after a round of high-stress gaming. "Sure you can play, if you don't mind the hand salsa." See also **Keyboard Plaque.**

Heat Index

The amount of response to an online discussion, usually due to the volatility of the subject. "The heat index on that Kurt Cobain topic is off the scale."

Height Technology

Silly engineers' euphemism for "ladder," as in "Can we get some height technology in here?"

High Dome

Synonym for "egghead." A scientist.

Hit Slut

A Webmaster who's obsessed with the number of times his/her site is accessed (or hit). A hit slut will do anything to shamelessly promote a site and wheedle links from other sites.

Hive Mind

The idea that a beehive is a collective, distributed being. The notions of hive mind and swarm behavior have become popular metaphors in digital culture. The dynamic and distributed Internet can be thought of as a hive mind. Kevin Kelly explores this notion in **Out of Control.** See also **Vivisystems.**

Hollywired

The community of companies using Silicon Valley technology to create media products with Hollywood production values. See also **Siliwood.**

Holy Wars

Perpetual Usenet discussions that never die; the arguments never vary, and no one's opinion ever seems to change. Holy wars are fought over abortion, gun control, Mac vs. IBM, Windows vs. DOS, and how much nudity to allow online.

Honky Handshake

When a peripheral device has standard handshake protocols and connects easily, "without a lot of street jive" (no complicated reconfiguring).

Hose and Close

When a phone tech support person spouts a bunch of jargon you don't understand, asks you to do a bunch of procedures you don't follow, and then says good-bye.

Hourglass Mode

Waiting in limbo for some expected action to take place. Refers to the hourglass icon used in Microsloth Windows. "I was held up at the post office 'cause the clerk was stuck in hourglass mode."

Huge Pipes
A high-bandwidth Internet connection. "CU-SeeMe doesn't look half-bad...if you've got huge pipes."

IC/OOC

[In Character/Out of Character]

Used in MUDs or other online role-playing when someone is moving in or out of character. "OOC: I have to leave soon."

Idea Hamsters

People who always seem to have their idea generators running. "That guy's a real idea hamster. Give him a raw concept and he'll turn it over 'til he comes up with something useful."

Identity Hacking

Posting on the Internet or a BBS anonymously or pseudonymously, or by giving a completely false name/address/phone with the intent to deceive. All these forms of concealing or playing with one's identity continue to be controversial in cyberspace. See also **Spoofing.**

ID10T
See **PEBCAK**.

Image Aspirations
Euphemism from plastic surgery for what bodily cosmetic changes one is willing to pay for. A digital imaging system is used to "realize" the image aspirations of a potential client and to generate a price list for the various desired body modifications.

IMNERHO
Net acronym for "In My Never Even Remotely Humble Opinion." Variant form of IMHO ("In My Humble Opinion") and IMNSHO ("In My Not-So-Humble Opinion").

Information Dominance

Military term for having superior intelligence and the ability to cripple an enemy's information infrastructure. "In the Gulf War, the coalition clearly had information dominance; in Somalia, it was Aideed." See also **Infowar**.

Information Gridlock

The traffic jams on the information superhighway that may eventually lead to full-blown Net collapse. See also **Web Brownouts**.

Infowar [or Cyberwar or Netwar]

Infowar is the use of information and information systems as weapons in a conflict in which information and information systems are the targets. Infowar is divided into three classes: Class I: personal privacy; Class II:

industrial and economic espionage;
Class III: global (nation-state vs. nation-state) information warfare. Infowar has also been referred to as "Third Wave Warfare." See also **Information Dominance**.

Intel
[from the sci-fi novel Snow Crash]
Term used to describe any useful information found in cyberspace. "Just got some cool intel on UNIX shortcuts from FringeWare."

Intellectual Gillnetting
The process by which Hollywood studios scoop up all conceivable intellectual rights to a given property by burying perpetual, universal "multimedia" rights within the contractual boilerplate.

Interrupt-driven
Term used to describe someone who moves through the workday responding to a series of interruptions rather than the work goals originally set.

In the Demo
Corporate slang for being a member of a targeted demographic group.

In the Plastic Closet
Said about someone who refuses to admit to having cosmetic surgery. "Is Tori Spelling in the plastic closet, or what!"

IQueue
The line of interesting email messages waiting to be read after one has deleted all of the junk and **floodgater** mail.

Irritainment

Entertainment and media spectacles that are annoying, but you find yourself unable to stop watching them. The O. J. trials were a prime example.

It's a Feature [from the adage "It's not a bug, it's a feature"]

Used sarcastically to describe an unpleasant experience one wishes to gloss over. "It's a feature," she sighed, after finding out that the elevator was broken and she'd have to climb five flights of stairs.

I-Way

Short form of information superhighway.

Jargonaut

A person who coins a piece of net slang/jargon with the express purpose of trying to get it into Jargon Watch. (This word was chosen during an impromptu contest run on alt.wired to coin such a term.)

J-culture

Shorthand for "Japanese culture." Also J-pop for "Japanese pop culture."

Jitterati

1. What the digital generation becomes after tanking up on too much coffee.
2. Fear and anxiety associated with not knowing the latest jargon, acronyms, and buzzwords of the Digital Revolution.

J-list

Shorthand/lazy netspeak for "journalist."

JOOTT [Just One Of Those Things, pronounced "jutε"]

Inexplicable computer problems that appear and then fix themselves (or are fixed by turning off the machine or reinstalling the software). No one knows what caused the problem or why it went away – it was a JOOTT.

JPIGs

The new generation of cybercops who want to remove pornographic images (often posted in JPEG format) from the Internet.

Juice a Brick

To recharge the big and heavy NiCad batteries used in portable video cameras. "You better start juicin' those bricks, we got a long shoot tomorrow."

Kevork [after Dr. Jack Kevorkian]

To kill something. "Look, kevork that project and let's go out for a beer," or "I read half the article, got bored, and kevorked it."

Kevorking is an example of a common method of slang creation: coining a slang term after a person or event in the news. **Going Postal, Perot, Rimm Job, Pulling a Caruso** (from former **NYPD Blue** actor David Caruso, meaning to quit when you're ahead), and **Pulling an O. J.** (to get away with murder), and **Bobbit** (to cut something short) are other examples. When one of these news-worthy events occurs, we often get a submission in the Jargon Watch mailbox within the week.

Keyboard Plaque

The disgusting buildup of dirt and crud found on computer keyboards. "Are there any other terminals I can use? This one has a bad case of keyboard plaque." See also **Hand Salsa**.

Keypal
Nickname for an electronic pen pal. "I've never met Mark, but he's a good keypal of mine."

Kill Your Babies
Term used in a production situation in which a piece of the work that one is particularly fond of must be removed. "We've run out of disk space for this presentation. Time to kill some of our babies in the sound files."

Kilroy Page
A corporate or personal Web page whose sole purpose is simply to say "Look, I'm here on the Web."

Knowbots

1. Software "agents" that can worm their way through a network looking for requested info. 2. Online know-it-alls. See also **Bots**.

When the subject of knowbots (see definition 2) came up in the Jargon Watch topic in the **Wired** conference on The Well BBS, three participants offered the following "Laws of Knowbotics": 1. Always answer any query or expressed need with a fact, regardless of whether that fact is relevant or true.[Joe Flower] 2. Always append your answer with some tangential or useless piece of knowledge that only you could find fascinating.[Daniel A. Murphy] 3. When a colleague presents you with a new idea, initiate the BTDT (Been There Done That) subroutine. For example, mention the paper you wrote "some time ago" that exhaustively explored the subject.[Mark Frauenfelder]

Kobrigram

A written legal threat sent in response to someone's online actions or statements. Coined in homage to Helena Kobrin, a Church of Scientology lawyer who's been threatening copyright and infringement lawsuits against those posting "secret" **CofS** documents.

Kodak Courage [from extreme sports]

An extra dose of courage and the tendency to go beyond one's usual physical limits when being filmed or photographed.

Kubris

An extreme form of arrogance found in multimedia auteurs who think they're Stanley Kubrick.

Last Mile

Refers to the copper wiring that currently connects most homes to the telephone and cable companies. Even though media and communications companies are busy laying high-bandwidth fiber-optic cable over their main networks, the cost in money and time of rewiring the last mile is a major stumbling block in getting high-speed connectivity into the home.
See also **Pulling Glass.**

Legacy Tech

Outdated wares that are basically obsolete but still too expensive to trash. Also called "heritage system."

Lemon Laundering
The fraudulent act of auto manufacturers repurchasing "lemons" and then putting them back onto the market without disclosing their lemon status.

Life Support
The condition of a business or project that is fighting for its life in the boardroom or the marketplace. "No, they're still in business, but definitely on full life support."

Link Rot
The process by which links on a Web page become obsolete as the sites they're linked to die or change location.

Loser Dust

Hollywood slang for the invisible substance that seems to cover some actors so that they can't do anything right. The opposite of fairy dust.

LRF Support

An official-sounding fictitious computer feature that can be used to test the knowledge of a **sales droid** or computer know-it-all. LRF stands for "little rubber feet." "Does this system come with LRF support?" LBL technology (for "little blinking lights") can also be used. See also **Sales Droid**.

In Rants and Raves, **Wired 2.10**, Kevin John Black, a San Francisco cab driver, tells the story of how he stumped an Apple employee he picked up. The Apple evangelist was waxing poetic about revolutionary new product, the Newton. As the guy exited the cab, Black asked, "Does it have LRF support?" After a moment of silence, he replied, "LRF? I'm sure we can look into it."

Magalog

A mail-order catalog that is disguised as a magazine in hopes of sucking in recipients. "Hey...this **International Male** 'magazine' is one of those stinking magalogs!"

Mail Bomb

The multiple sending of a single email message as an act of protest or harassment. "Some hackers mail bombed my account after I wrote a negative article about them." See also **Gang FAQ** and **Paste Bomb**.

Malicious Applet

See **Black Widow**.

Market-Leninism

The system replacing Marxism-Leninism as the new governing style of

China. Combines the ironfisted political rule of Leninism with the wide-open economic permissiveness of free-market capitalism. Think Singapore.

Martian Mail
An email message that arrives months after it was sent (as if it had been routed via Mars). See also **Martian Packet** and **Zen Mail**.

Martian Packet
Strange fragments (data packets) of electronic mail that turn up unexpectedly on the wrong computer network because of bogus routing. Also used for a fragment that has an altogether unregistered or ill-formed Internet address.

Masthead Envy

Jealousy toward those who appear on a publication's masthead before you. See also **Egosurfing**.

MCI Project

A low-budget entrepreneurial effort financed by one's network of friends and family. "Pam's latest CD is completely an MCI project." See also **Ribs 'n' Dick**.

Meatspace

One of the many slang terms for the physical world as opposed to the virtual. See also **Carbon Community, Facetime, F2F,** and **RL**.

Media Contamination

Term used by Los Angeles Superior Court Judge Lance Ito in referring to the possible tainting of the O. J. Simpson jury by exposing themselves to media coverage.

Meltomedia

See **Blendo**.

Met Ed

Hip-hop slang for getting f***ED over, dissED, screwED, or rippED off. "Boy, I met ed on that Newton. It's a piece of crap!"

Midair Passenger Exchange

Grim air-traffic-controller-speak for a head-on collision. Midair passenger exchanges are quickly followed by "aluminum rain."

Monday Morning Webmasters

Coworkers (often from the sales department) who magically appear after the unveiling of a new Web site. Although previously unavailable for assistance or insight, they suddenly show up and say "How long would it take to...?" or "You know what would be really cool...."

Monitor JuJu

See **Geekosphere** and **Monitor Pets**.

Monitor Pets

The little trinkets, mementos, and toys that decorate one's computer monitor. Objects that are imbued with spiritual or superstitious significance are sometimes referred to as "monitor juju." See also **Geekosphere**.

MorF?
Online shorthand for "Male or Female?"
Posed as a question in online chat rooms
as conversants try to determine the sex
of other occupants. "Sandy – MorF?"
Often responded to with age and
geographical location: "F/24/Cleveland."
See also **SorG?**.

Mouse Potato
The online, wired generation's answer to
the couch potato.

Muchomedia
Playful variation on "multimedia."
See also **Blendo**.

Multimediocrity
Boring, poorly done CD-ROMs,
multimedia Web sites, and the like.
See also **Shovelware**.

NASCII
Porno images rendered in simple text (ASCII).

Nervous Net
An approach to robotic control that relies on networks of transistors, capacitors, and other basic electronics to orchestrate autonomous lifelike behaviors, as opposed to neural nets that use high-end digital hardware and software. See also **Photovore.**

Nesting
What Jay Chiat, of the Chiat/Day advertising agency, accuses his employees of doing if they sit at the same table more than two days in a row.

Netsploitation Flick

Any one of the Hollywood films about the big, scary Internet (**The Net**, **Hackers**, etc.).

Netwar

See **Infowar**.

Neurobotics

The emerging science and technology of biological computing. Where neurobiology and robotics meet.

Neurohackers

Amateur scientists who experiment with do-it-yourself brain tinkering, using entrainment devices (also called "brain toys"), biofeedback machines, magnetic stimulation, and EEG mapping software. See also **Wireheading.**

NIMQ [pronounced "nihm-kyoo"]

Acronym for "Not In My Queue." Said in response to suggestions of additional tasks or projects when one is already feeling overwhelmed. Similar to the more common "It's not **my** job."

NLB [Nonlinear Behavior; from chaos theory]

Used to describe overly emotional or irrational "flaming" on the Net. "That gun control topic is being overwhelmed by NLB."

Nooksurfer

Someone who frequents only one or two newsgroups or BBS topics, or just logs on to answer email, never daring to venture out into the big waters of the Net.

Notwork

A network in its nonworking state.

Nox and Sox
Two classes of pollutants (nitrogen oxides and sulfur oxides) traded like commodities by the Regional Clean Air Incentives Market in Los Angeles.

NRN [No Response Necessary]
A proposed email convention that can prevent endless back-and-forth acknowledgments: "Thanks for the info." "You're welcome, hope it helps." "Thanks, again." And so on. By putting NRN at the bottom of your mail, you absolve the receiver from having to reply, thus saving precious email time.

This term was coined by **Wired** editor Kristin Spence in an effort to propagate it as an email convention. Unfortunately, it hasn't caught on yet.

Nut Cluster

What you get on college campuses when a group of obsessive MUD (multi-user dimension) players takes over an entire computer cluster, or a row of terminals, to hold an all-night MUD session. See also **Furverts.**

Nutraceutical

A food with pharmaceutical properties (such as beta-carotene). Lobbyists are now petitioning the FDA to recognize this as a new category – a cross between a food and a drug.

Nyetscape

Nickname for AOL's less-than-full-featured Web browser.

Nym-rod

An individual (or subculture) that insists on turning every multiword term into an acroNYM (ATM, SMTP, 3Do, NII, T2, ADSL, etc.).

Object Value

In industrial design, a measure of consumers' immediate desire for an object, even before knowing or understanding what it does. "That eMate has killer object value."

Off the Grid

Euphemism for being off of the Net. "Sorry I didn't email you last week, I was off the grid in Mexico." Also refers to people who live out in the country and generate their own power.

Ohnosecond

That minuscule fraction of time in which you realize that you've just made a BIG mistake. Seen in Elizabeth P. Crowe's book **The Electronic Traveller.**

OIC

Online shorthand for "Oh, I see."

Open Collar Workers

People who work at home or tele-commute. See also **SOHO.**

Paintmonkey

A person with a less-than-glamorous entry-level computer graphics job. A paintmonkey may spend months working on a single second of digitized film footage, painting mattes, or doing monotonous touch-ups.

Panarchy

A political unit or state in which everyone has power.

Panic Merchants

Businesses, media outlets, and moralistic groups that make their living by exploiting common fears and anxieties. AIDS, escalating crime, ecological doomsday, porn on the Internet, and destructive rap lyrics are some of the fears that panic merchants have marketed.

Paste Bomb

A random or unrelated piece of data that is cut from one's hard drive and pasted into an online conversation. Meant to entertain, infuriate, and befuddle online conversants. Sci-fi author and Net spider Bruce Sterling is a notorious paste bomber.
See also **Mail Bomb.**

Playgrounds

Indoor pay-to-play kid parks, such as Discovery Zone, that substitute for what previous generations got for free at now mostly extinct public playgrounds.

PEBCAK

Tech support shorthand for "Problem
Exists Between Chair And Keyboard." In
other words, there's nothing wrong with
the computer, it's the user that's
causing the problem.

Techies are a frustrated, often arrogant lot. They've
submitted numerous acronyms and terms that poke fun
at the clueless users who call them up with frighten-
ingly stupid questions. Another variation on the above
is **ID10T**: "This guy has an ID-Ten-T on his system."

Percussive Maintenance

The fine art of whacking the crap out of
an electronic device to get it to work
again. This may be old military slang but
it is equally applicable to the world of
computer hardware.

Someone reported on the sci.electronics newsgroup
that several studies have shown that connectors/con-
nections are the most failure-prone element in an electronic system. Bad connections weaken, solder cracks,

connectors and switches oxidize, potentiometers get dusty, and so on. A well-placed whack can often jar the connection back into service.

Permalancer

A permanent freelancer. A person continuously hired by the same company on a per-project basis who lives a benefits-free existence.

Perot

To quit unexpectedly, as in "My cellular phone just perot'ed." Refers to H. Ross Perot's unexpected and temporary withdrawal from the 1992 presidential campaign. See also **Kevork.**

Peter Panning

Reattaching the shadow to an object in a graphics application such as Photoshop. Named after the boy who asked Wendy to sew his shadow back on.

This piece of jargon prompted a letter from a woman who took offense at the fact that this process would be called Peter Panning and not Wendying: "As usual, a woman does all the work and a man gets the credit."

Pharming
[short for "pharmaceutical farming"]

The process of genetically engineering crops to protect them or their consumers from disease. Example: Researchers at Texas A&M and Tulane have genetically altered potatoes to include antigenic material from **E. coli** bacteria, one cause of diarrhea. Theoretically, consumption of such potatoes would serve the dual purpose of feeding people in developing countries and vaccinating them against this pathogen.

Photovore

Term used in BEAM robotics (a minimalist, biologically inspired approach to robotics) to refer to an autonomous bot that seeks out a light source to energize its solar power panels.

Picasso Porn

The scrambled images on adult cable channels that can sometimes be seen (and heard) by nonsubscribers.

Pickling

Archiving a working model of an old computer to read data stored in that computer's format. Apple Computer has pickled a shrink-wrapped Apple II in a vault so that it can read Apple II software in the distant future.

Ping Flooding

The malicious flooding of an IP address with ping (test) packets, which cause lag for anyone accessing that address.

Pixel Shim

A small (usually invisible) graphic used in an HTML document to make the page format the way you want it. "I had to use a pixel shim to get the type to space correctly." Now rendered obsolete by the introduction of Netscape's <SPACER> tag.

Plug

A temp worker or a new addition to a work staff to cover work overflow. "He's a plug for Jean until she gets back in June."

Plug-and-Play

A new hire who doesn't need any training. "The new guy, John, is great, he's totally plug-and-play."

Point-of-purchase Politics

Cause-related marketing, such as that used by Benetton and The Body Shop.

Pomosexual

People who claim to be bisexual because they think it's hip but would never have a sexual encounter with someone of the same sex.

PONA [Person Of No Account]

Someone who is not online.

Port-per-pillow

The goal of some universities to get network connections into the bedrooms of every student on campus.

Power Luser

Computer user with the uncanny ability to screw things up so badly that either the damage is irrevocable or restoring from the last backup is the only hope. From the old hacker term **luser** (loser + user).

Prairie Dogging

When someone yells or drops something loudly in a **cube farm** and everyone's heads pop up over the walls to see what's going on.

Print Miles

The distance covered between a desk and a printer shared by a group of users in an office. "I think I've traveled enough print miles on this job to qualify for a free vacation."

Pseudophone

A pay phone that looks like a real RBOC phone but is owned by a smaller phone company that charges exorbitant fees for long-distance calls.

Pulling Glass

Laying down fiber-optic cable. See also **Dark Fiber, Data Freight,** and **Last Mile.**

Quants

Short for quantitative analysts, the Wall Street financial nerds who use complex mathematics to devise far-out derivatives and other esoteric investments. Also known as "math jockeys", "rocket scientists", or "quarks."

Quarterly Charm Deficiency
[QCD]

An emotional disorder that arises in executives at the end of each fiscal quarter.

Rasterbator

A compulsive digital manipulator.
A Photoshop abuser. See also **Bit Diddling**
and **Cornea Gumbo.**

Realies

Location-based entertainment that
combines elements of videogames,
movies, and amusement park rides.
Virtual reality rides or narratives.
See also **Barfogenesis** and **Smart Seats.**

Render Farm

A networked collection of computers
(usually more than six) set aside
exclusively for the purpose of
rendering animations.

Render Wander

To walk around the building chatting to people while the progress bar of **AfterEffects/Premiere/Infini-D** (etc.) makes its ponderous journey across the screen. Compare with **Graybar Land**.

Ribs 'n' Dick

A departmental budget with no fat for pet projects. "We've got ribs 'n' dick and we're supposed to find 20K for memory upgrades." See also **MCI Project**.

Rimm Job

Having the wool pulled over one's eyes by a bogus academic study masquerading as legitimate science. Named after Marty Rimm, author of the dubious "cyberporn" study from Carnegie Mellon that became a controversial **Time** magazine cover story.

RL
Shorthand for "Real Life" (as opposed to the virtual worlds of cyberspace). Also IRL ("In Real Life"). "What do you do IRL?" See also **Facetime, F2F,** and **Meatspace.**

Road Builders
The people in an organization who come along behind the **arrow shooters** and pave the way for profitable applications.

Road Rage
The increasing phenomenon of excessive anger and sometimes violence among motorists.

Road Warriors
Salespeople whose office is their laptop and cellular phone.

ROM Brain

Someone who spews forth ideas and opinions but can't seem to accept any input from the outside world.

Router Droppings

The inclusions added to email messages by routers when a server or recipient cannot be found. Cryptic and foul looking, they require a kind of scatological analysis to find what the router problem was. Also called "daemon droppings."

Rumorazzi

Writers of various back-page "industry insider" columns in computer trade journals. Dedicated to collecting and reporting (and sometimes debunking) various rumors and secrets within the industry. "Be careful at Comdex; you never know where the rumorazzi may be lurking."

Sacrificial Host

A computer server placed outside an organization's internet firewall to provide a service that might otherwise compromise the local net's security. Spotted in Cheswick and Bellovin's **Firewalls and Internet Security.**

Sales Droid

Hacker pejorative for a computer salesperson. See also **LRF Support.**

Salmon Day

When you spend the entire day swimming upstream only to get screwed in the end.

Screenagers

Term used to refer to either wired teens or the much-sought-after marketing demographic of 18–24 year olds who grew up in front of a TV/computer screen.

Scud Memo

Poorly composed office memo, letter, or email that does more damage to the sender's reputation than to the intended target(s). See also **Career-Limiting Maneuver.**

Seagull Manager

A manager who flies in, makes a lot of noise, shits all over everything, and then leaves.

See Through

An office building, built during an economic growth spurt, that remains unrented (and therefore can be seen through as one passes by). "That building in Clarendon was a see through for over three years."

Send Storm

The result of being deluged with private chat messages while trying to do something else online. "Sorry, I'm currently the victim of a send storm. I'll be with you in a moment." On AOL, the same thing is called "being IMed to death" (IM stands for "Instant Message," AOL's private chat feature).

Serendipity Search

An Internet search in which you end up finding interesting and valuable things that were not in the original search. Searching willy-nilly. "I found this really cool site on Tiki collecting during a serendipity search."
See also **Domain Dipping.**

Shen [short for "shenanigan"]

A harmless prank or practical joke. Used on the alt.shenanigans newsgroup. "That was a cool shen you pulled on Eric."

Shopper-lifting

When a store's electronic scanner prices an item higher than the price noted on the store's shelf or in an advertisement. It's currently not clear how much shopper-lifting is by design and how much is inadvertent.

Shoulder Surfing

Looking over someone's shoulder to get his or her credit card or phone card number or access password.

Shovelware

A CD-ROM title or Web site that contains mostly preexisting material. Also called a "kitchen-sink title." See also **Multimediocrity.**

Silicon Alley

The area of lower Manhattan that has a high concentration of computer and multimedia firms.

Siliwood

Short for "Silicon Hollywood," the coming convergence of movies, interactive television, and computers. See also **Hollywired.**

Single-systemitis

Term used to describe the condition of people who use only one computer system, refusing to learn or even acknowledge the worth of any others.

SITCOMs [Single Income, Two Children, Oppressive Mortgage]

What yuppies turn into when they have children and one of them stops working to stay home with the kids. The true martyrs of Reaganomics, as character-ized in **The Economist.**

Slag

1. To bring a network, especially a LAN, to its knees by overloading it with data traffic, as in "We slagged the Net last night by playing **Spectre** while the MIS department was trying to reindex the accounting files." 2. The irrelevant,

uninteresting material one must bust through to get to the rich information ore (sometimes called "bitslag"). "I tried to find that reference to the BookSite security breach, but only found slag." See also **Bitslag** and **Ping Flooding**.

SloGo [short for "slogan + logo"]

Corporate slogans used repeatedly, in a manner similar to a logo. Nike's "Just Do It" and AT&T's "You Will" are prime examples.

Small Indulgence Syndrome

Spending money on small luxuries and frivolous purchases when hard economic times prevent the purchase of big ticket items such as cars, houses, and expensive recreation. Coined by cultural trend watcher Faith Popcorn.

Smart Seats

The seats found in VR entertainment venues that are equipped with motion bases and wired to respond to actions on the computer screen. See also **Barfogenesis** and **Realies**.

Sociomedia

Computer media used for social purposes, as a means of exchange, for collaboration, and for the social construction of knowledge. Computer conferencing is a perfect example of sociomedia. The term was suggested by hypermedia theorist Edward Barrett in his book of the same name.

Softlifting

1. The pirating of software for individual use (as opposed to commercial piracy for profit or corporate piracy for free distribution within an organization).
2. The process of interrogating computers on a network, gathering intelligence on what software is being run on the machines, and then reporting that finding back to a machine gathering such information.

SOHO

Acronym for "Small Office, Home Office." See also **Open Collar Workers.**

SorG?

Online chat shorthand for "Straight or Gay?" See also **MorF?.**

Spamdexing
The practice of entering the same keyword multiple times in a Web page (in the META tag) to force it to the top of search results in a search engine.

Spamming
1. Flooding Usenet newsgroups and email boxes with commercial ads. Made popular after the infamous "Green Card" spam was sent to some 9,000 newsgroups.
2. [rare] Filling someone's head with information of questionable value or content. "Some jerk on AOL started spammin' me about Rush Limbaugh's political genius." See also **Velveeta**.

Spew
The global media feed. Used by Neal Stephenson in his story of the same name in **Wired 2.10**.

Spoofing

1. Assuming the identity of an authorized user in an attempt to gain access to a computer system. 2. The interception, alteration, and retransmission of data in an attempt to fool the recipient. 3. In MUDs/MOOs and graphical virtual worlds, causing to appear on-screen messages that are not attributed to one's character/avatar. See also **Identity Hacking**.

Sprawl Sites

Web sites that seem to go on forever, choked with content and hard to navigate.

Square-headed Girlfriend (or Boyfriend)

Another word for a computer. The victim of a square-headed girlfriend is a "computer widow."

Squirt the Bird
To transmit a signal up to a satellite. "The crew and talent are ready; what time do we squirt the bird?" See also **Juice a Brick.**

Stalkerazzi
Paparazzi who will go to just about any lengths to get the shot they desire.

Stalker Site
A Web site created by an obviously obsessed fan. "Have you seen that Gillian Anderson stalker site? The guy's got like 200 pictures of her!"

Starter Marriages
Short-lived first marriages that end in divorce with no kids, no property, and no regrets.

Start-outs

Enterprises that begin inside big companies and then receive funding from venture capitalists to launch them into new and separate businesses.

Strangelove Ocean
[from the movie Dr. Strangelove]

Ecology slang for an ocean in which higher species appear to be largely extinct – making it look like a nuked wasteland – as evidenced by low or absent primary productivity. Coined by paleo-oceanographer Ken Hsu.

Stress Puppy

A person who seems to thrive on being stressed out and whiny. "I'd like to work with Patrick, but he's too much of a stress puppy...everything's a crisis."

Super Searcher

See **Cybrarian.**

Swiped Out

An ATM or credit card that has been rendered useless because the magnetic strip is worn away after extensive use at gas pumps, grocery checkouts, and bank machines. "We wanted to stop for suds, but my card was swiped out so I couldn't get cash."

Synthespians

Synthetic actors. Term used in 3D computer animation to describe sophisticated human forms that can be imported into a virtual world or film. Also called "electronic puppets" and "vactors" (virtual actors).

Techflation
Military term for the growing cost of high-tech weaponry, which runs about 3.4 times the annual rate of inflation.

Technohedonists
People who always rush to promote the latest digital technology as the "next big thing," regardless of the appropriateness of that technology or its market.

Technopolis
The sum total of the technological infrastructure of a society.

Telecrats
High-ranking telecom executives who are more like government bureaucrats than businesspeople.

Telephone Number Salary
A salary (or project budget) that has seven digits.

Teturist
The repetitive stress injury one gets after long-term play of highly addictive puzzle games like **Tetris.**

Thong-α-thon
Any B movie whose major selling point seems to be women in thong bikinis.

Thrashing
Clicking helter-skelter around an interactive computer screen in search of hidden buttons that might trigger actions. (Found in the manual to the CD-ROM game **Myst.**)

Throbbers

Animated icons that are used to replace the "meteor shower" icon in Netscape Navigator. Taken from the nickname given to the original Netscape logo, which appeared to throb during document transfers. New icons, such as the J. R. "Bob" Dobbs throbber, are currently traded over the Net.

Thumb Candy

A fast-action videogame requiring lots of button pushing. Similar to **Twitch Game**.

Time Porn

Popular entertainment, such as TV shows like **Seinfeld** and **Friends**, in which people never seem to have anything to do except hang out. They tease us with the forbidden leisure we all covet, but can't have.

TORI
[Totally Obvious Rapid Information]
An information spew, usually from a **sales droid,** of completely rudimentary and useless information. Designed by people to snow others into believing they know what they're talking about when they obviously don't. "Did you catch the TORI from that Circuit City guy?"

TOSsεd Out
Ejected from the chat rooms on AOL for violating the Terms of Service (TOS) agreement. The ejection-happy arbiters of taste who do the TOSsing are sometimes referred to as cybercops.

Tourists

People who take training classes just to get a vacation from their jobs. "We had about three serious students in the class; the rest were tourists." In hacker slang, a guest on a system is also called a tourist.

Toy Value

Useless gewgaws in a program or product. "The animation screens in this backup program may have some toy value, but they slow everything down to a crawl."

Tract Mansions

Large, expensive homes built in tractlike developments by the nouveau riches. Commonly seen in the mountain states and West Coast digital boomtowns.

Treeware

Hacker slang for documentation
or other printed material. See also
Dead Tree Edition.

Triple-dub

An abbreviated way of saying **www**
(double-u, double-u, double-u) when
speaking a URL. "Hey, check out this
cool Web site at triple-dub dot
neowobbly dot com."

Trog Mode

A round-the-clock hacking session in
which your eyes get so tired you have
to turn off the lights and toggle the
monitor into reverse – white letters on
a black screen. Programmers in trog-
lodyte mode often prop themselves
up with stimulants, loud music, and
periodic outbursts of colorful language.

Trolling

On Usenet newsgroups, the act of baiting readers, especially newbies, with a post that's designed to incite a large volume of angry responses. Posts that scream out racists epithets are common trolls. Posting "Nine Inch Nails TOTALLY sucks!" to the alt.music.nin newsgroup would be a troll.

Tweak Freak

A computer techie who's obsessed with finding the root of all tech problems, regardless of the relevance of doing so. A tweak freak might spend hours trying to track down something that could instantly be fixed by reinstalling the software.

Twitch Game

A computer or arcade game that's all hand-eye and little brain. Similar to **Thumb Candy.**

Umfriend

A sexual relation of dubious standing. "This is Dale, my...um...friend...."

Under Mouse Arrest

Getting busted for violating an online service's rules of conduct. See also **TOSsed Out.**

Uninstalled

Euphemism for being fired. Heard on the voicemail of a vice president at a downsizing computer firm: "You have reached the number of an uninstalled vice president. Please dial our main number and ask the operator for assistance." See also **Decruitment.**

Vactors
See **Synthespians.**

Value Subtracted Reseller
A company that buys components from other companies and puts them together into a system that's less than the sum of its parts. Opposite of value added reseller.

Vampire Time
A time schedule in which one sleeps all day and haunts clubs and coffeehouses at night. Refers to writers, artists, slackers, club kids, and other bohemian types. Also "vampire hours."

Vanity Domain
A noncommercial Internet domain that has the same name as its owner (e.g., sean@sean.com).

Velveeta

A Usenet posting, often commercial in nature, excessively cross-posted to a large number of newsgroups. Similar to spam, although that term is often used to describe an identical post that's been loaded onto lots of inappropriate newsgroups, one group at a time (rather than cross-posted). See also **Spamming.**

Vivisystems

Large complex systems, both artificial and natural, that exhibit lifelike behaviors. The Internet, **SimCity,** and a tropical rain forest are all vivisystems. Coined by Kevin Kelly in **Out of Control.** See also **Hive Mind.**

Voice Jail System
A poorly designed voicemail system that has so many submenus one gets lost and has to hang up and call back.

VR Sickness
See **Barfogenesis**.

Vulcan Nerve Pinch
A condition caused by the taxing hand position required to reach all the appropriate keys for certain commands. For instance, the warm boot for a Mac II involves simultaneously pressing the Control key, the Command key, the Return key, and the Power On key.

WAD Widows

Significant others who hardly ever see their mates because they are so busy creating WAD scenario files for use in the games **DOOM, DOOM II,** or **Heretic.**

Waitbuster

Checkout counter display stand that entices one to buy, buy, buy. Also called a "shelftalker."

Wankware

Another term for X-rated software.

WAW [Waiter-Actor-Webmaster]

Term used to describe fly-by-night graphic designers/Web consultants trying to cash in on the Web boom. "Can you believe they hired that clueless WAW for $90K a year?!"

Way New Journalism

Phrase coined by writer Joshua Quittner to update Tom Wolfe's "new journalism" for the digital age. Where new journalism was about having fun with the facts, using an intimate voice, and taking risks, way new journalism adds a greater element of surprise (through the use of additional media), a more immediate and interactive voice, instant feedback (through online chats and email), links to relevant support materials and shorter more dramatic storytelling. The "way" in "way new" comes from "information superhighWay." See also **Bitraking**.

Webbelganger

A person who comes up in an online search but is not the person you're searching for.

Web Brownouts
Network slowdowns that are occurring as more and more people access the Internet with higher speed connections and more requests for capacity-hogging multimedia files. See also **Information Gridlock.**

Webmaster
The name given to the person in charge of administering a World Wide Web site.

Some terms that originally appeared in the Jargon Watch column have become so universal that it seems foolish to include them in this book. We took out a number of them (e.g., **FAQ** and **Infobahn**), but chose to leave Webmaster in as an example of jargon that whizzed through **Wired** on its way to mainstream usage.

Webmistress
A female Webmaster.

Webwench

An employee given all the responsibility for a Web site without any of the authority (the opposite of a Webmaster).

Why Bother

Coffeehouse slang for a decaf coffee with nonfat milk. "One large latte why bother and a bagel...comin' up." See also **Jitterati.**

Wireheading

The very dangerous thrill-seeking practice of hooking electrodes to one's temples to deliver small controlled doses of electroshock therapy. A related practice involves shocking the genitals. Warning: Don't try this at home! See also **Neurohackers.**

World Wide Wait

The real meaning of "WWW."

Xerox Subsidy

Euphemism for swiping free photocopies from a workplace.

YMMV [Your Mileage May Vary]

A popular qualifier simply meaning that the outcome may be different under different conditions. "This shareware program worked fine on my machine, but YMMV."

YODA [Young Opinionated Directionless Artiste]

Arts majors and related hangers-on who sit in coffeehouses voicing strong opinions and perennial wisdom while exhibiting little direction or effort to actually make a difference.

Yuppie Food Coupons

The ubiquitous $20 bills spewed out of ATMs everywhere. Often used when trying to split the bill after a meal: "We all owe $8, but all anybody's got is yuppie food coupons."

Zεn Mαil

Email messages that arrive in one's mailbox with no text in the message body. See also **Martian Mail.**

Appendix

Jargon/Slang Resources
฿✲✲ks

Barry, John A. **Technobabble,** Cambridge, MA:
MIT Press, 1991.
A critical and humorous look at how technobabble (computerese mixed with marketspeak)
is invading the English language.

Dalzell, Tom. **Flappers 2 Rappers:
American Youth Slang,** Springfield, MA:
Merriam Webster, 1996.
A trip through 20th-century youth slang.
Besides the obvious (**jive, beat, hippie, hip-hop,
college**) there's also the lingo of slot-car racers,
yo-yo enthusiasts, child tramps, marble players,
and others.

Eble, Connie. **Slang & Sociability,** Chapel Hill:
University of North Carolina Press, 1996.
College slang guru Connie Eble (author of
College Slang 101) examines the process by

which slang is created and propagated and the role it plays in a social fabric.

Hale, Constance. **Wired Style: Principles of English Usage in the Digital Age**, San Francisco: HardWired, 1996.
Wired's other guide to the language of digital culture. Covers context and usage and defines common terms, acronyms, organizations, and digital subcultures. A companion interactive Web site is available at **www.wiredstyle.com/**.

Kelly-Bootle, Stan. **The Computer Contradictionary**, Cambridge, MA: MIT Press, 1995.
A cynical lexicography in the spirit of Bierce, including "**bit bucket,** a binary spittoon"; "**email,** a picturesque novella listing the ... gateways, nodes, mailers, and protocols responsible for mangling the appended one-line message"; and "**multimedia,** an application attack on all five senses, especially smell."

Raymond, Eric S., ed. **The New Hacker's Dictionary,** Third Edition. Cambridge, MA: MIT Press, 1996.
The definitive dictionary of hacker jargon and slang. **THD** grew out of the legendary Jargon File begun at Stanford and circulated through hacker culture in the '70s and '80s.

Thorne, Tony. **The Dictionary of Contemporary Slang,** New York: Pantheon, 1990.
Over 5,000 colloquial expressions from the United States, Great Britain, Australia, the Caribbean, and elsewhere.

Web Sites

The Alternative Dictionaries
www.notam.uio.no/~hcholm/altlang/about.html
A collaborative Internet research project to collect slang and "dirty words" from around the world.

The Free Online Dictionary of Computing
wfn-shop.Princeton.EDU/foldoc/sites.html
A handy online reference of computer and Internet terminology, including some slang.

The Jargon File
www.ccil.org/jargon/jargon.html
Eric Raymond's online, constantly updated version of **The Hacker's Dictionary.**

The Totally Unofficial Rap Dictionary
www.sci.kun.nl/thalia/rapdict/
Excellent dictionary of rap/hip-hop and other urban street slang.